PERSONAL POETRY

Edited By Jenni Harrison

First published in Great Britain in 2022 by:

Young Writers
Remus House
Coltsfoot Drive
Peterborough
PE2 9BF
Telephone: 01733 890066
Website: www.youngwriters.co.uk

All Rights Reserved
Book Design by Ashley Janson
© Copyright Contributors 2021
Softback ISBN 978-1-80015-747-7

Printed and bound in the UK by BookPrintingUK
Website: www.bookprintinguk.com
YB0492F

FOREWORD

For Young Writers' latest competition This Is Me, we asked primary school pupils to look inside themselves, to think about what makes them unique, and then write a poem about it! They rose to the challenge magnificently and the result is this fantastic collection of poems in a variety of poetic styles.

Here at Young Writers our aim is to encourage creativity in children and to inspire a love of the written word, so it's great to get such an amazing response, with some absolutely fantastic poems. It's important for children to focus on and celebrate themselves and this competition allowed them to write freely and honestly, celebrating what makes them great, expressing their hopes and fears, or simply writing about their favourite things. This Is Me gave them the power of words. The result is a collection of inspirational and moving poems that also showcase their creativity and writing ability.

I'd like to congratulate all the young poets in this anthology, I hope this inspires them to continue with their creative writing.

CONTENTS

Independent Entries

Harrington Smithers (9) — 1

Bill Quay Primary School, Bill Quay

Nikita Mohan (10)	2
Jacob Topping (10)	5
Charlie Allison (10)	6
Jake Davidson (10)	8
Ella Paul (10)	9
Layla Evans (10)	10
Imogen Olsen (10)	11
Christopher Grieves (11)	12
Jack Millin (10)	14
Fraser Ritson (10)	15
Nieve Cryer (10)	16
Martha Harkin (10)	17
Keeron Scarfe (10)	18
George Chapman (10)	19
Charlie Lancelot George (10)	20
Eric Barrett (10)	21
William Brookes (10)	22
Daisy Mancini (11)	23
Grace Sanderson (10)	24
Elliot Robson (10)	25
John-James Hobbs (10)	26
Ruby Corr (10)	27
Evie Summers (10)	28
Ethan Nevins (10)	29
Olivia Harvey (10)	30
James Reisner (10)	31
Bentley Diamond (11)	32
Finn Herald (10)	33
Sam Masoabi (10)	34

James Pagan (11) — 35

Clyst Heath Nursery & Community Primary School, Clyst Heath

Lily Ahokovi Day (10)	36
Olivia Blell (10)	38
Finley Lock (7)	40
Isabella Newcombe (9)	41
Hattie Marriott (7)	42
Poppy Bennett (10)	43

Great Alne Primary School, Great Alne

Emma Willmott (10)	44
Isla Law (10)	46
Anna Holder (9)	48
Chloe McStrafick (9)	50
Belinda Carr (9)	51
Ilani Watters (10)	52
Burhan Faisal (10)	53
Hugo (9)	54
Alfie Swingler (10)	55
Blythe Reid (11)	56
Traviss Belcher (9)	57
Evie Carr (10)	58
Phoebe Shuttleworth (10)	59
Ethan Woodfield (10)	60
Aiden Tremble (10)	61
Ollie Wilson (10)	62
Michael Woodfield (9)	63

Penruddock Primary School, Penruddock

Ella Tiffin (10)	64
Cerys Robinson (10)	65
Caitlin Byrne (10)	66
Cailtin Doyle (8)	67
Anna Hamilton (9)	68
Hayden Bond (10)	69
Liam Winden (9)	70
Sophia Teasdale (8)	71
Romaine Hodgson (8)	72
Max Nicot (7)	73
Lewis Hebdige (8)	74
Jonathan Tiffin (7)	75
Hector Ashburner (10)	76
Ben Windross (7)	77
Josie Teasdale (7)	78
Isla Bond (7)	79
Logan Airey (9)	80
Isabelle Binks (9)	81
Oscar Wood (9)	82
Josh Parker (8)	83

South End Junior School, Rushden

Millie Beevers (8)	84
Chloe Vintner (10)	85
Jessica Man (8)	86
Oscar Zielinski (9)	87
Bernadette Boulton (8)	88
Kharis Miller (8)	89
Lily Dearn (9)	90
Lily Dickins (10)	91

The Godolphin Junior Academy, Slough

Umar Sajjad (7)	92
Wania Waqas (10)	94
Safa Hussain (7)	95
Fariah Amara Khan (9)	96
Duaa Mir (7)	97
Ariel Mavure (8)	98
Aliyyah Hussain (9)	99
Jahanzaib Hussain (7)	100
Amna Saleem (10)	101
Aadam Qazi (8)	102

The Rosary Catholic Primary School, Stroud

Janiel Ugbede (6)	103
Sean C. Ike-Nwofor (9)	104
Mia Webb (7)	105
Emma Neale (7)	106
Peniel Ugbede (7)	107
Nadia Denis (7)	108
Katy Watt (7)	109
Abbie Watt (5)	110

Woodlands School, Great Warley

Elliott Carter (10)	111
Amelia Parker (10)	112
Madeline Bolesworth (10)	114
Thomas William Ashby (10)	115
Athena Bloom (10)	116
Kieran Chantler (10)	117
Oliver Kerley (9)	118
Bethany Conti (10)	119
Joel Adegbite (11)	120

THE POEMS

This Is Me!

This is me
I never want a pea
I like snacks
Like crisps in their packs

I was born in December
Not November
I don't like potatoes
Or smelly old toes

I'm not fast
But I like a blast
This... is... me!
I never want a pea!

Harrington Smithers (9)

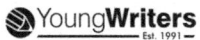

How To Create A Nikita Cake

To create me in the form of a delicious cake, you will need:
A sprinkle of yellow sand
A splash of blue sea
Seven spoons of sweet sugar
A spot of cinnamon
Half a spicy red chilli
A small pinch of lemon juice
Bamboo for a panda cub
A dog's loving lick
A dash of adventure
Oven mittens
A gooey chocolate cake

Preparation
Be careful not to steal the bamboo
From the baby panda
It might cry if you do that
You don't want that

This Is Me - Personal Poetry

Venture far, to the beaches of Hawaii
And put your sand and sea
In a container
But be careful not to let them touch
In case of contamination

Now you are ready to create your own Nikita Cake

In two separate bowls,
Add a sprinkle of yellow sand and a splash of blue sea

Next, add a spot of cinnamon
And seven spoons of sweet sugar

Add in the bamboo for a panda cub and a dog's loving lick
Followed by my love of all animals

After stirring for 111 seconds (111 is my favourite number)
Add in half a spicy red chilli and a small pinch of lemon juice

Finally, put the creation into the oven to add some of my extra warmth
After 10 years take the Nikita cake out of the oven
And leave her to cool

Congratulations! If you followed the recipe you should have created a Nikita Cake.

Nikita Mohan (10)
Bill Quay Primary School, Bill Quay

This Is Me

To create me you will need:
A room full to the brim with footballs
A cone with a summit of delicious strawberry ice cream
A pair of far-fetched football boots
A dash of merriment and mischief
10lb of a Newcastle supporter
A pinch of foolishness
A sprinkle of hatred for Sunderland Football Club

Now you need to:
Add 10lb of Newcastle supporter
Stir thoroughly for a minute in a room full to the brim with footballs
Whisk while adding a cone with a summit of delicious strawberry ice cream
Now apply a pair of far-fetched football boots
Add a dash of merriment and mischief
Cook until ready and add a sprinkle of hatred for Sunderland Football Club

This is me!

Jacob Topping (10)
Bill Quay Primary School, Bill Quay

A Recipe For Success

Ingredients:
A handful of footballing ability
A six box of McNuggets
A pinch of leadership
And a dash of bad-temperedness
40 grams of confidence
A tin of noodle hair
And you can't forget a splash of Xbox

Preparation:
Preheat the oven to 130 degrees celsius
Buy your McNuggets,
Open your McNuggets,
Put them on a tray and cook for 30 minutes at 90 degrees celsius,
Butter your pan

Method:
First, get a bowl and put your leadership and bad-temperedness in it,
Next, pour your Xbox into the same bowl and mix until thick,
After that, place your noodle hair in your pan and add a pinch of footballing ability.

Cook until golden brown,
Then put the confidence in the oven for an hour,
After that, add your McNuggets to the pan and stir for 5 minutes.
Finally, cook all of this in the oven for two hours and place your confidence on top and enjoy.

This is me!

Charlie Allison (10)
Bill Quay Primary School, Bill Quay

How To Bake Jake

To make me you will need:
1 whole duck
10 teaspoons of gaming
5kg of fish loving
2 tablespoons of homework
2 grams of creativity
7 teaspoons of early rising
1 pound of kindness
1 tonne of enthusiasm

First, add a whole duck to your bucket of sushi,
Then pour in two tablespoons of homework,
Add 10 teaspoons of gaming,
Then mix 5kg of fish loving,
2 grams of creativity also put in,
7 teaspoons of early rising,
Followed by 1 tonne of enthusiasm,
Last, but not least, add 1 pound of kindness.
Mix until thick then put in the oven for around 120 months.
Then you've got me.

Jake Davidson (10)
Bill Quay Primary School, Bill Quay

How To Make Me?

You will need:
A spoonful of excellent eventing
A dash of art
Half a cup of Brussels sprouts - not!
10 pounds of fun and cheekiness
Sprinkles of resilience
And a cup of happiness

How to make me:
First, add 10 pounds of fun and cheekiness,
Now add a spoon full of excellent eventing,
Stir in a dash of art and a pinch of dedication,
Next, pour a cup of happiness into the mixture and put it in the oven until you start to see little bubbles of joy
Allow to cool and then top with a sprinkle of resilience.
This is me!
Enjoy!

Ella Paul (10)
Bill Quay Primary School, Bill Quay

Make Me

To create me you will need:
A tablespoon of mischief,
A slab of hot cheesy pizza,
A jar of dreams and goals,
A sprinkle of fun,
A teaspoon full of energy,
A handful of happiness.

Now you will need to:
Add a jar of dreams and goals,
Start mixing in a sprinkle of fun,
Stir roughly while adding a teaspoon full of energy,
Next, add a handful of happiness,
And now chop in one slab of hot cheesy pizza.
Cook until perfection and can see steam coming out,
Then sprinkle over 1 tablespoon full of mischief and fun.

Layla Evans (10)
Bill Quay Primary School, Bill Quay

This Is Me, Imogen

To create me you will need:
A handful of strawberries and blueberries,
Many oranges
A dash of a messy bedroom,
A teaspoon of happiness,
Two teaspoons of fun,
10lb of sweets.

Now you need to:
Take in 10lb of sweets,
Add in the two teaspoons of fun,
Then mix until it makes a batter,
Next, add the teaspoon of happiness,
With a dash of a messy bedroom,
Then add the oranges,
Mix until the batter is tall,
Cook until sweet and polite,
Add the strawberries and blueberries on top to decorate.

Imogen Olsen (10)
Bill Quay Primary School, Bill Quay

This Is Who I Am

I have lost my nana, my grandad
And two of my three siblings.

This is me
I am a chatty,
I'm funny,
I'm friendly and a gamer

This is my family,
My brother James,
My mam Lindsay,
And my dad Michael

This is me
I have family in Dubai, Sardinia and Dunfermline

This is me
A footballer,
An online super spender,
A Netflix binge-watcher

This is me
I'm an all America lover

With the exception of
American football.

Christopher Grieves (11)
Bill Quay Primary School, Bill Quay

Jack's Recipe

Ingredients:
A handful of footballing ability
A six box of hot wings
A pinch of hot-headedness
A teaspoon of sarcasm
And a heart full of hopes and dreams

How to assemble:
First, take a teaspoon of sarcasm and a pinch of hot-headedness, let that sit for ten years.
Next smack in a six box of hot wings to the mixture as well as a handful of footballing ability.
Finally, add in a brain full of knowledge and a heart full of hopes and dreams.
Stir until sky blue.
Enjoy!

Jack Millin (10)
Bill Quay Primary School, Bill Quay

This Is Me, Fraser

I'm kind, I'm smart, I'm a hard-working dart
A machine that gets things clean,
A brother to a brother
And a son to my mother

I live in a big house that luckily has no mouse,
A room to myself and a big bookshelf

I have a dog called Buddy and a sister and a dad
I also have a big personality but sometimes in a mood

I'm determined to be happy and positive always and
Be like the human dictionary in my school.

This is me!

Fraser Ritson (10)
Bill Quay Primary School, Bill Quay

How To Make Me

To make me you will need:
1 teaspoon of daydream,
A sprinkle of curiosity,
10 grams of forgetfulness,
1 loaf of bread,
1 jar of peanut butter,
1 large hook,
1 baby sloth.

Now you need to:
Add 10 grams of forgetfulness and 1 loaf of bread into a bowl,
Mix it in a jar of peanut butter and 1 large hook,
Stir in a baby sloth and add in a sprinkle of curiosity and a teaspoon of daydream,
Cook at a low temperature and leave to cool.

Nieve Cryer (10)
Bill Quay Primary School, Bill Quay

How To Make Me

How to make me:
70lbs of imagination,
A gaming set-up,
A cheese-stuffed crust, 11-inch meat feast pizza,
A pinch of fun,
5 litres of Lucozade,
An old blue hat.

Instructions:
First, add 4 litres of the Lucozade into a pan with 70lbs of imagination,
Then stir whilst adding the 11-inch meat feast pizza and the old blue hat,
Once stirred add the remaining 1 litre of Lucozade and a gaming set-up,
Serve with a pinch of fun.

Martha Harkin (10)
Bill Quay Primary School, Bill Quay

My Lovely Life

I walk the dog,
I feed the fish,
I sleep like a log,
Before making a wish.

Every day,
I'll cook some food,
Scrummy or yummy,
I'll eat it all too.

I have good friends,
They're amazing to me,
I'm amazing to them,
While we're out on the streets.

I love to joke,
And cheer up cries,
It doesn't always work,
But I'm delighted to try.

Keeron Scarfe (10)
Bill Quay Primary School, Bill Quay

How To Make Me

To make me you will need:
A room dedicated to football,
10lb of exercise
A pinch of school
A clash of happiness,
A lump of pizza,
A piece of ginger.

Now you need to:
Add the 10lb of exercise,
Mix in the pinch of school and a pinch of ginger,
Stir everything while adding a lump of pizza,
Finally, add a room dedicated to football and leave it in the oven for 20 minutes.
This is me.

George Chapman (10)
Bill Quay Primary School, Bill Quay

This Is Me

T all I am in size,
H ungry and miserable I am inside.
I 'm fond of my fluffy dogs Milo and Ralph
S creaming I tend to do and loud it makes me.

I adore KFC and the way it fills me
S miling I like to do, especially when I find a cool rock.

M y love for peanut butter is beyond compare
E nglish is my main language and England is my home.

Charlie Lancelot George (10)
Bill Quay Primary School, Bill Quay

Eric's Poem

I am a kind dog
I am a brave tiger
I am a friend
When I am with my friends I become enveloped in happiness
I am a funny clown
I am a caring and creative person
I am a helpful friend
The wind whistles through my ears as I walk with my kind and caring grandad
I am a silly sausage
I am a fun-filled house
I am a pizza eater
I am an Axolotl lover
I am a book reader.

Eric Barrett (10)
Bill Quay Primary School, Bill Quay

William's Cheesy Pizza

A teaspoon of curiosity
A cheesy pizza
1,000 grams of cat-loving
A bucket full of fun
10 grams of sadness
1,000 grams of kindness

How to make William's pizza
First up take a teaspoon of curiosity
Next, add in 1,000 grams of cat-loving
Then add a bucket full of fun
After add 10 grams of kindness
Then add a cheesy pizza.
This is me!

William Brookes (10)
Bill Quay Primary School, Bill Quay

Daisy Soup

To make Daisy soup you will need:
7 teaspoons of weird,
Half a cup of sadness,
1 full cup of glee,
2 grams of shyness,
3 cups of kindness,
1 pinch of outgoing,
1 full bowl of friendship then mix until strong,
3 buckets of creativity,
1 crying apple,
2 Halloween pumpkins,
2 dog treats,
Add 10 big strands of clumsy spaghetti.

Daisy Mancini (11)
Bill Quay Primary School, Bill Quay

This Is Me

T his is me,
H ate people that hurt children or animals.
I love spending time with my family
S eeing people lonely makes me upset.

I love playing with my little sisters
S pending my money on perfume and clothes.

M aking cookies with my mam
E veryone says I am polite and caring.

Grace Sanderson (10)
Bill Quay Primary School, Bill Quay

Me, Elliot Robson

E ats pasta,
L ord of the Rings,
L ikes Fortnite,
I am a friend,
O ath keeper,
T urtle lover.

R esilient,
O wl-like,
B lue eyes,
S tuffed crust extra-cheese pizza,
O rigami is boring to me,
N ever intolerant.

Elliot Robson (10)
Bill Quay Primary School, Bill Quay

This Is Me

T he best food is KFC
H ebburn Town football player
I am lightning when running
S isters are the best.

I support Newcastle United
S hopping with my mam and dad is the worst.

M onkeys are the best animal
E very day I am a family guy.

John-James Hobbs (10)
Bill Quay Primary School, Bill Quay

This Is Me

T he sea scares her with its mysteries
H er eyes are dark brown in the daylight
I know she loves books
S he is very sensitive

I know she adores crystals
S tar patterns are her favourite

M essy but caring
E mbarrassed sometimes.

Ruby Corr (10)
Bill Quay Primary School, Bill Quay

This Is Me, Evie

T his is me,
H as a terrible sweet tooth
I love baking
S ometimes quite chatty.

I enjoy reading and learning about WWII,
S ometimes quite annoying.

M ost of the time rage quits (my time always gets wasted),
E vie is my name!

Evie Summers (10)
Bill Quay Primary School, Bill Quay

Ethan's Fire Rap

My name is Ethan and I love football,
I am switched on going down the line - offside!
When I'm on fire I sprint to the net.
And pull the trigger - goal!

I hate spiders they're one of my biggest fears,
I hate their eight long creepy legs
Going up my ceiling.

Ethan Nevins (10)
Bill Quay Primary School, Bill Quay

This Is Me, Olivia

A spoonful of reading,
A cup of art.

A kilogram of creativity,
With a dash of animal-loving.

A gram of shopping,
And a sprinkle of kindness.

A drop of confidence,
With a dash of hard work.

Mix it all together,
This is me.

Olivia Harvey (10)
Bill Quay Primary School, Bill Quay

This Is Me

T all in size
H ates losing
I am bored easily
S ometimes fidgety

I am always shaking somewhere
S ometimes I am mad at small things

M um says I'm a picky eater
E asily distracted.

James Reisner (10)
Bill Quay Primary School, Bill Quay

This Is Me

I'm a terrific footballer,
Hater of homework
I am often scared
Silly a lot

I like my hair, fluffy and soft
I'm sad sometimes

I'm mad when my computer is not turning on
Every time I sing, it makes me feel good.

Bentley Diamond (11)
Bill Quay Primary School, Bill Quay

This Is Me

First, take a bowl full of cheese and tomato pasta,
Mix in a sprinkle of fun, a teaspoon of caring and loving,
A jar full of energy with a cluster of friends and family,
Add to the oven at 150 degrees.
Until golden brown

This is me.

Finn Herald (10)
Bill Quay Primary School, Bill Quay

This Is Me, Sam

T iny in comparison,
H ates maths,
I love video games,
S uper planner,

I am a lovely mate,
S neaky family member,

M ultiple talents,
E xtra charming.

Sam Masoabi (10)
Bill Quay Primary School, Bill Quay

This Is Me

T all,
H arry Potter fan,
I am a dazzling dancer,
S trong as a striker

I love fun Fridays,
S uper scooter rider

M usic-related
E nergised by sports.

James Pagan (11)
Bill Quay Primary School, Bill Quay

My Big, Independent Life

My big independent life,
Is going to be the best,
My big independent life,
Will be better than the rest.

I don't know what's going to happen,
I don't know what it's going to be,
Because it's in my future,
That's something I can't see.

My life is going to be happy,
My life is going to be sad,
My life will be full of hope
When things are very bad.

I am going to live my life
And follow my dreams
And every wish I make
Is going, to be honest, and clean.

I'm going to open up my heart
To others in need

I'm going to sow happiness
With a little hope seed.

My big independent life
Is full of family and friends
And I'm going to keep them close
Until the very end.

Lily Ahokovi Day (10)
Clyst Heath Nursery & Community Primary School, Clyst Heath

In My Pocket

In my pocket
I have the world
I keep it safe
From the cold

In my pocket
I have my sword
I keep it hidden
Until I'm bored

In my pocket
I have my friends
I keep them close
Until the end

In my pocket
I have my cats
They're funny and furry.
And I once gave them top hats

In my pocket
I have my family

My sister and mum are strong
But my dad is manly

In my pocket
I have my wand
It makes me, me
When I raise it in my hand.

Olivia Blell (10)
Clyst Heath Nursery & Community Primary School, Clyst Heath

All About Me

I like to go to the park,
But only when it is not dark.
My friends really like football
But sometimes they play rough
I think I need to be a little bit more tough!
I like to play with my sister
I'm so glad she isn't a mister.
When at the park I sometimes get hungry
I can tell as my tummy gets grumbly!
Cuddles are the best
As it always helps me rest,
My family are the best.

Finley Lock (7)
Clyst Heath Nursery & Community Primary School, Clyst Heath

Me

My hair is brown
My eyes are too
I love reading Dork Diaries
Perhaps you should try it too
I love to ride my bike
But going up steep hills is quite a hike
I really really love school
And I love swimming in the pool
Playing with my friends is always the best
But when you're 'it' it's always a pest.

Isabella Newcombe (9)
Clyst Heath Nursery & Community Primary School, Clyst Heath

Mecipee Recipe

H elpful, I like to help people and be kind and thoughtful
A rtistic, I enjoy being creative
T alented, I've got loads of medals from sports.
T errific teamwork is my favourite.
I mpressive, I am imaginative.
E xcitable, I have loads of energy.

Hattie Marriott (7)
Clyst Heath Nursery & Community Primary School, Clyst Heath

Autistic

A utism is a part of me
U sually, I feel different
T hrough happy and sad
I wish I wasn't sometimes
S ome things make me sad
T hough they shouldn't
I am autistic
C an you see me?

Poppy Bennett (10)
Clyst Heath Nursery & Community Primary School, Clyst Heath

My House In Autumn

The trees blowing in the whistling wind,
Fills my heart with cheer,
The crunching of the leaves beneath my feet,
Is music to my ears.
The dogs are barking,
Amazon's here.
Oh please be quiet,
My poor old ears.
Now they are digging,
To try and find the mole,
Uh oh, dad's shouting,
"I've just filled that hole!"
The dogs are barking,
"Oh not Amazon again! What's Mum bought now,
A jumper, a handbag, a pen?"

As night-time arrives,
Peace is finally here,
Just the sound of the owls,
The badgers,
And the distant deer.

The dogs aren't barking,
They have started to tire,
Now they're all curled up by the flickering fire.

Today has been manic,
But one thing's for sure,
My family mean the most, and nothing matters more.
Being honest to my friends,
And my family too.
Having fun until the day ends,
Baking cakes until the day's through,
Singing, dancing and acting,
Are what make me feel free,
This poem is about
What makes me, ME!

Emma Willmott (10)
Great Alne Primary School, Great Alne

Save The Beaches

As I pace across the shore
Sand sinks between my toes.
Waves racing like lions
Wrestling their foes.

As I climb the ladder
And step out onto the pier.
I'm greeted with a spectacular view
And the sound of seagulls crying, filling my ears.

How I love beaches,
If only they were clean.
How I wish I could stop it
The problem facing them is so mean.

But to stop it I need you to follow this precise advice
So reduce your carbon footprint.
Don't litter
Recycle when you can
So we can rescue our beaches.
With this simple plan
Remember this message

And do what I say,
To save our beloved beaches
And you will thank me someday.

Isla Law (10)
Great Alne Primary School, Great Alne

Poem Of Me

I would love a unicorn,
But I wouldn't mind a fawn,
I am adventurous, loving, and kind,
There is so much in my mind,
My favourite subject is art,
And I have a giant heart,
Animals are my thing,
I'm always in the mood to sing,
I love to play the guitar,
And even in the car.
I like to imagine things,
I'm a quick reader,
And I am a good leader,
I've got one sister,
And I am a wisher,
I am fast and sporty,
I am not naughty,
I love the beach,
I like honey,
And I'm going to get a bunny.

My name is Anna,
And that's the poem of me.

Anna Holder (9)
Great Alne Primary School, Great Alne

The Things I Love

I love climbing mountains that reach high up in the sky,
The birds that soar above me,
The clouds that make me cry.
The sunset in the violet sky,
The peaceful sound of wildlife awaking.

I love my cats that always snuggle up on mats,
No mouse or louse survives in this house.
They are the meat stealers,
They are flashes of colour whizzing down the hall and up the stairs.

I love all things Harry Potter,
My favourite house is Gryffindor,
In Quidditch, they love to score.
I love the excitement, the danger and the happiness.

All these things I love,
Just like a dove.

Chloe McStrafick (9)
Great Alne Primary School, Great Alne

Trying

If there was one thing I had to choose to do for my life,
I would choose football because I could storm onto the pitch
As a substitute at the last minute of the game
Then score the winning goal,
I was sure that the goal would give my team the trophy.
And the sound of the crowd screaming my name.
I ran around celebrating and felt really amazed.
Whenever I feel worried
I look in the sky before the crowd go quiet.
The sun was burning my back
I really didn't feel well
But I did always try to score another goal
Until I did.
Trying will always pay off.

Belinda Carr (9)
Great Alne Primary School, Great Alne

Myself

Skin as golden as a fantasy treasure chest,
Silky hair as brown as melted chocolate on a summer's day.
Eyes as a magnificent hazel shade that glimmers in the sun.
With the extravagant energy of a fluffy rabbit,
With wonderful raindrops dripping down.
My fall on such a lovely day.
Drawing and baking delicious cookies for everybody to enjoy, because doing that is my true passion.
Twirling in the winter snow, and acting as if I was on a dancing show.
Then everything on my mind just goes away as if it was the start of a new day.

Ilani Watters (10)
Great Alne Primary School, Great Alne

I Can Be Anything

As kind as a good friend,
As silly as a baby and as
Dirty as a fully grown muddy carrot.
As high as a mountain touching the bright blue sky.
I eat, I sleep, I work and I love to play with my kind friends.
As hungry as a lion and as funny as a joker.
I sometimes get angry but enough is enough I tried so much not to get angry.
I love my mum's chocolate cake but I'm very sorry, I go crazy with Oreo milkshakes.
I will take my time writing my poem but I will not take my time rhyming my poem.
I can be anything.

Burhan Faisal (10)
Great Alne Primary School, Great Alne

About Me

I'm as lazy as a seal, slopping on a rock before sliding back into the water.
I'm as crazy as an ostrich, believing it can fly.
I'm like an elephant, always eating, but as thin as a homeless lizard.
I'm as cheeky as a crow, looking for food.
I'm as wise as an owl, but with no clues.
I'm like a gerbil, small and fast like the whirlwind I am.
I'm as silent as a mouse, waiting for a chance to scram.
This is me.
I'm as happy as can be, chilling with my friends.

Hugo (9)
Great Alne Primary School, Great Alne

This Is Me

Cooking makes me happy,
Chocolate cake covered in raspberry sauce.
My strawberry ice cream sundae is better than yours

Cooking makes me happy,
Lemon and lime jelly needs to get in my belly.
Pineapple on pizza is best of all.

Cooking makes me merry,
My mayonnaise tuna pasta,
Is better than Nan's juicy lasagna.

Cooking makes me merry,
Tender gammon roast dinner followed by
Peanut butter cupcakes to add some glamour.

Alfie Swingler (10)
Great Alne Primary School, Great Alne

Let Out The Anger

Sometimes I feel
I can't conceal
The anger deep inside.
It starts to burn and
Twitch and turn,
Like the waves of
A violent tide.
I hold my mouth
Try to keep it in
But then it bursts
Right out.
I can't conceal it any longer,
So your tears will cause a drought.
I fight as much but it's not enough
I'm sorry it didn't work,
It is time to go,
So goodbye foe.

This argument was so berserk.

Blythe Reid (11)
Great Alne Primary School, Great Alne

I Am

I am as brave as a bear facing a bully,
As healthy as a kitten being active every day,
As smart as an owl teaching and learning,
As helpful as a dog but also having fun,
As happy as a seal dancing in front of loads of people,
As excited as a boy who just had his birthday,
As kind as a warm heart making someone's day,
As special like everyone in their own way,
As funny as a fish gulping with laughter,
I can be anything.

Traviss Belcher (9)
Great Alne Primary School, Great Alne

What Makes Me, Me

Cooking a cake for me to eat,
Play with my dog and put up my feet.

Creating a dance with all my friends,
And have a party until the day ends.

Toasting marshmallows, sitting round the campfire,
And watching TV until my eyes tire.

Sing a song all day long,
Sit in my room and hear the church bells dong.

Doing gymnastics it's all so fun,
And having a water fight in the midday sun.

Evie Carr (10)
Great Alne Primary School, Great Alne

The Show

Like a bird she flies over the jump
She sharply zooms around
The corner hit her head
Up high looking for the
Weaving poles.
She swiftly twists around the poles.

She pelts towards the sensor
Within her eye is worriedness
But her owner gives her comfort
So she sprints towards it
Bravely running down
She races to the finish line
And she makes it.

Phoebe Shuttleworth (10)
Great Alne Primary School, Great Alne

Gross Me

Gross slime and other sticky stuff,
Popping into buddles,
My fingers getting sticky and slimy,
That's just gross sticky me.

Sticky Play-Doh on the couch,
It's falling on the floor, Mum screaming
"Pick it up now!"
"I'm too lazy," I say
Mum says, "I don't care."
That's just gross, sticky, lazy me.

Ethan Woodfield (10)
Great Alne Primary School, Great Alne

This Is Me

A poem can make you laugh,
Like you're tickling a giraffe.
It can make you feel angry,
Like a raging gorilla,
Looking for his dinner.
It can make you feel lonely,
Like a sloth,
That has just been hit by a cloth.
It can make you curious,
Like you are furious.

Aiden Tremble (10)
Great Alne Primary School, Great Alne

What Makes Me, Me

I am as musical as a dog as it barks in the park,
I am a full-time gamer sitting on my comfy sofa,
I am excited for my birthday,
I am a curious caterpillar who is always wondering,
I am a kind and caring cat with long whiskers, tiny paws and the smallest nose in the world.

Ollie Wilson (10)
Great Alne Primary School, Great Alne

Christmas

I love ripping Christmas presents open and discovering what's inside.
The feeling of it makes me glow inside.
I like when it's Christmas Eve.
But when it's gone I cry and sob inside.
My feelings go and flow away until I wait for next Christmas Day.

Michael Woodfield (9)
Great Alne Primary School, Great Alne

The Way I Am

Energy is my thing like a bursting bottle of Coke that has just been shaken.
As graceful as a swan, I spin and leap to the music.
Running like a greyhound, I sprint to the finish,
This is me.
Curious and adventurous like a majestic lion stalking its prey, I wait.
I am as comforting as a mug of hot chocolate and as cuddly as a cat.
This is me.
Like a monkey I hang upside down in a tree, swinging from vine to vine.
This is me.
I am a goal shooter, as fast as an arrow from a bow, I catch and throw.
This is me.
Like popcorn in a microwave, I pop and grow every day.
This is me.

Ella Tiffin (10)
Penruddock Primary School, Penruddock

This Is Who I Am

Energy is what I own,
Like a bursting bottle of lemonade.
Magic thrives in my self-esteem.
A curled up ball of imagination waiting to explode.
This is me.
A courageous adventurer like a mountain goat,
Crossing a steep, rocky cliff,
As fast as a greyhound sprinting the last leg.
Running is my superpower, life is my mission.
Swinging on branches and leaping off trees,
Like a delighted monkey in a top hat.
This is me.
Like a bee, I am a surging bubble of yellow,
Buzzing from flower to flower,
A nectar thief waiting for the next flower to bloom.
This is me.

Cerys Robinson (10)
Penruddock Primary School, Penruddock

All About Me

I am as chatty as a parrot,
I am always on my feet like a crab that never rests,
I am as loud as a foghorn,
I can be as calm as a tree on a summer's day,
I am as tall as a giraffe,
I am a fish darting through the sea,
I am as fast as a sheepdog leaping through glossy fields,
I am as deft as a squirrel munching through acorns and scuttling up trees,
I am as brave as a lion hunting through the savannah,
My hair is melted chocolate oozing off my head,
My eyes are chocolate cupcakes with green and blue icing.

Caitlin Byrne (10)
Penruddock Primary School, Penruddock

Nature On A Tree

I'm as pink as a flamingo,
As tropical as a fresh peach,
And as white as a fluffy cloud,
Growing beautifully and peacefully on a melted chocolate tree.
I can be found in a blue wet soaking river by a tree blowing me to the floor,
I can be as white as Santa's beard, as white as snow.
I could be as purple as lavender,
As blue as the midnight sky,
I can be coloured blue, lavender, pink and white
My petals are as smooth as a white piece of paper.

Cailtin Doyle (8)
Penruddock Primary School, Penruddock

Who I Am

I am as comforting as a snuggly cat,
I am as cheeky as a monkey.
Like a dog, when I'm outside I will run forever.
I am a bubbling whirlpool, spreading the laughter,
I am a snake coiled up ready to pounce
My eyes are blue beach balls.
I am sunshine beaming every day,
I am as sweet as a violin singing a lovely melody.
I am as chatty as a dolphin,
This is me.

Anna Hamilton (9)
Penruddock Primary School, Penruddock

This Is Me

I am as energetic as a shaken bottle of Coke bursting out,
I am as happy as a hippo rolling in the mud,
This is me,
I am as curious as a cat stalking a mouse,
I am as comforting as a mug of hot chocolate on a cold winter's night,
This is me,
I am as noisy as a parrot squawking at the top of my lungs,
I could walk the Grand Canyon on a tight rope,
This is me.

Hayden Bond (10)
Penruddock Primary School, Penruddock

My Farming Life
A kennings poem

- **F** ast runner
- **A** pple eater
- **N** ever gives up
- **T** ractor fan
- **A** mazing biker
- **S** illy child
- **T** own hater
- **I** ncredible helper
- **C** ow feeder

- **F** armer's best friend
- **A** nimal lover
- **R** eliable farmer
- **M** orning moaner
- **E** nergetic driver
- **R** eliable farmer.

Liam Winden (9)
Penruddock Primary School, Penruddock

Who Am I, Riddle

I am younger than three years old,
I am a blonde baby boy.
I am as loud as a car on a racing track,
I hate fruit,
I am as small as a pebble rolling down a hill,
I am as cute as a puppy playing,
I am as mischievous as a kitten,
My hair is as yellow as the sun shining.
Who am I?

Answer: Lucas my baby brother.

Sophia Teasdale (8)
Penruddock Primary School, Penruddock

This Is Me

T iny as a book
H appy as a dog playing with a new toy,
I 'm as nosy as a bear
S miley as an upside-down rainbow.

I 'm as calm as a sloth,
S neaky as a snake.

M y hair and eyes are as brown as wood
E veryone says I'm kind, this is me.

Romaine Hodgson (8)
Penruddock Primary School, Penruddock

Guess Who I Am?

I am as happy as a monkey eating juicy bananas.
I am as heavy as a penguin, sliding around.
I am as flexible as a lion eating its yummy desert.
I am as creative as a bat flying.
I am as colourful as a hippo in mud.
I am as tall as a horse lying down.
I am as handsome as a flamingo sleeping.

Max Nicot (7)
Penruddock Primary School, Penruddock

What Am I?

I am as cute as a tiger sleeping peacefully.
I am as hungry as a child.
I am as funny as a human.
I am as fast as a cheetah running after its prey.
I am as black as a raven.
I am as furry as a lion.
I am as sleepy as a baby.
I am as silent as a feather falling from the sky.

Lewis Hebdige (8)
Penruddock Primary School, Penruddock

What Am I?

My habitat is fun and busy.
It's noisy too with all the mooing.
I am as quiet as a mouse hunting for cheese.
I am as big as a blue tractor.
I am as fast as a cheetah chasing its prey.
I am as good with football as Harry Kane.
Who am I?

Answer: Me.

Jonathan Tiffin (7)
Penruddock Primary School, Penruddock

This Is Me

I am a grumpy sloth or a happy seal,
I am a tortoise when it's hibernating,
I am as tall as a giraffe,
My chocolate-eating kills are Olympian.
I am a farmer feeding pigs jokes instead of apples,
I am an amber traffic light wanting to turn green.
This is me.

Hector Ashburner (10)
Penruddock Primary School, Penruddock

Boa Constrictor

I am as big as a lion,
I am as scary as a crocodile.
I am as camouflaged as a chameleon,
I am as long as a hose pipe.
To catch my food I strangle my prey then I swallow it whole.
I am big, scary, slippery, scaly, cold and very long.
What am I?

Ben Windross (7)
Penruddock Primary School, Penruddock

This Is Me

I am as noisy as a lion roaring,
I am as calm as a sloth sleeping.
I am as peaceful as a koala eating leaves,
I am as cute as a bunny eating carrots
I am as caring as a nurse.
Who am I?

Answer: A leopard.

Josie Teasdale (7)
Penruddock Primary School, Penruddock

This Is Me

I am as fluffy as a sheep in the middle of winter,
My fur is as soft as silk.
I am more adorable than a little rabbit,
I am as small as a pebble lying on the beach
I am like a cheetah
I like pouncing
This is me.

Isla Bond (7)
Penruddock Primary School, Penruddock

Logan's Poem

I am as bouncy as a kangaroo bouncing in the heart of Australia,
I am as chatty as a parrot in the Amazon rainforest,
I am as fast as a jumpy bumpy rabbit,
I am as funny as a baboon's bum in the big yellow sun.

Logan Airey (9)
Penruddock Primary School, Penruddock

This Is Me, Isabelle

I am a lion ready to pounce,
I am as sneaky as a tiger,
I am as excited as a lion cub,
I am as bored as a busy bee,
I am as slow as a sloth,
My eyes are as blue as a butterfly.

Isabelle Binks (9)
Penruddock Primary School, Penruddock

Oscar

O ptimistic
S o fast I'm as speedy as Sonic
C reating and destroying pizza
A lways being brilliant
R iding on my bike like a car, this is me.

Oscar Wood (9)
Penruddock Primary School, Penruddock

Josh's Superpowers

I can read like a lion
Chasing its prey
I'm a computer whizz-kid.
I'm a hugger and I give the best hugs.

Josh Parker (8)
Penruddock Primary School, Penruddock

Orange Me

I have beautiful orange locks of hair,
I have furry orange eyebrows,
I have spiky orange eyelashes,
And a million orange freckles all over my body.
People call me ginger, carrot top, redhead, orange fruit and ginger nut.

But I am more than orange...
I can swim as fast as a shark,
I am Roald Dahl writing imaginative stories.
I can paint beautiful art like Picasso.
I am an Olympic cyclist riding gracefully on my bike,
I am a gamer, a fidget person, a sister and a friend.
I am orange on the outside but so much more on the inside.

Millie Beevers (8)
South End Junior School, Rushden

This Is Me, Chloe

My name is Chloe Vintner
It's just coming up to winter.
I love the cold and snow
It gives me get up and go.
I love the outdoors
And stroking my dog's paws.
I'm very artistic
I try to make my drawings realistic.
I am passionate and hard-working
Looking for challenges wherever lurking.
One day I hope to travel
As a vet where adventures unravel,
This is a bit about me
I am Chloe V.

Chloe Vintner (10)
South End Junior School, Rushden

I Enjoy Being Me

When I dance I like to prance,
When I sing I like to spring.
When the sun comes up I like to hear the drums,
When I'm not proud I like to feel like a cloud.
When I pretend I'm a bunny I like to think it's funny,
When it's loud it's not proud.
When it's loud its not proud,
When it's light it makes it bright
When I'm me it's always good to be.

Jessica Man (8)
South End Junior School, Rushden

The Seasons

The sky is blue, the air is misty.
The flowers are ocean blue and smell really good.
The air is hot, the sun is orange and the weather is really sunny.
The sun is cloudy and the sun's not that bright.
And all the leaves come tumbling down.
And now it is winter
The sky is all white and the surface is covered with frosty white clouds.

Oscar Zielinski (9)
South End Junior School, Rushden

This Is Me

This is me,
Starting with a B,
Ending with an E,
Like doing a tap dance,
Many after school dances.

This is me,
Used to do swimming,
Now I can't swim,
Luckily we do swimming lessons at school,
Now a confident swimmer.

This is me,
Hopefully, you understand,
But you can be totally different.

Bernadette Boulton (8)
South End Junior School, Rushden

Peppermint Stick

I took a lick of a peppermint stick,
And oh it tasted yummy.
It used to be a peppermint stick but it's in my tummy
It was so yummy,
That the peppermint stick was as big as a little lollipop.

Kharis Miller (8)
South End Junior School, Rushden

Mummy And Me

Mummy and me love each other every day,
Mummy and me like to play.
We laugh together and play games,
We also love to explore.
We like to be cooks,
And we love reading books.

Lily Dearn (9)
South End Junior School, Rushden

Shimmering Diamonds

Shimmering diamonds in the night,
Shimmering diamonds oh so bright,
I'll be with you not forever
Forever me and my bestie will be together forever.

Lily Dickins (10)
South End Junior School, Rushden

Me, Myself And I

I am like the filling of a sandwich,
I have one older brother,
One older sister,
One younger brother,
One younger sister,
I am the middle child and everyone says I am special.
I love cruising in the car,
Going on outings, eating out at restaurants and watching movies on a Friday night.
I study really hard and like reading stories, especially the ones which make me laugh.
I have lots of energy and enjoy riding my scooter and going to my swimming classes.
I am very inquisitive and am interested in what's happening around me.
I love mangos, especially the sweet ones from Pakistan.
I love cream cakes and tasty desserts.
I enjoy playing computers games and chilling at home.

I am happy, joyful, caring, and loving.
I am Umar and I love to have fun!

Umar Sajjad (7)
The Godolphin Junior Academy, Slough

Wania Da Great

Listen up all of you,
Because I'm going to tell you something you never knew.
There's a girl called Wania.
But she is not a princess so she hates tiaras,
She loves to eat sleep and game.
But she is fine stroking a vicious lion's mane.
She may be slow but she is smart.
I would like to see her brilliant art.
She is cunning, even more than a spy.
But in big gatherings, she may be shy,
But let me tell you what her life was.

About 6 years ago she came in darkness,
All alone, only her parents.
But she had many unknown talents
Joined Warden Hill later.
Months later
As she was tasked many favours,
But let's just pause there.
Maybe later we can tell you as an older sister
How she needed to share.

Wania Waqas (10)
The Godolphin Junior Academy, Slough

This Is Safa

Safa was born on 4th May,
Her brother's favourite Star Wars day.
She is funny,
She is kind
And if you shout she will mind.
She loves cookies and milk
And loves making clothes out of silk.
She loves her family,
But she can get mad
When nobody plays with her she gets sad
Playing with dolls is Safa's hobby
She has all of them including Barbie,
Safa is loved by everyone.
She is the only girl.
And is lots of fun.

Safa Hussain (7)
The Godolphin Junior Academy, Slough

The One, The Only, Me

I'm teeny tiny but mighty.
Curly, quirky and a little kooky.
Love playing with words and strumming my guitar,
Doodling and dabbling,
With my enormous imagination.
Cartwheeling and handstands,
Just call me an acrobat.
I'm always full of smiles and sunshine
Even on the gloomiest of days.
I know that's a lot but hey that's just me!

Fariah Amara Khan (9)
The Godolphin Junior Academy, Slough

I Am Duaa Mir

I am Duaa Mir
I am kind,
I am confident,
I am special in my family,
I am hardworking,
I am proud of myself,
I am safe with my mum and dad,
I am glad to be me, the colour of my skin,
I am very blessed to have two sisters Ajwa and Zoha,
I am so thankful for my God for this life.

Duaa Mir (7)
The Godolphin Junior Academy, Slough

Summer Day

Summer day in summertime,
A bright beautiful girl standing on the sand.
Lots of blue water and the sunset,
Crabs and clam, snails and octopus
Rise up to the top made the sand angels,
Bright sun shining on the ground
What a lovely face you have
Bright, big and round and brave as a lion.

Ariel Mavure (8)
The Godolphin Junior Academy, Slough

Phenomenal Aliyyah

A wesome listener
L ikeable learner
I nterested in detective books
Y ellow sunflowers are my favourite
Y es to unicorns, butterflies and roses
A s bright as the shining stars in the sky
H appy as can ever be.

Aliyyah Hussain (9)
The Godolphin Junior Academy, Slough

This Is Me

Jahanzaib is kind,
And Jahanzaib is funny.
He has a family,
A family of 5,
Not the oldest
Zap, bang, kapow, boom.
And I like seedless winter melons.
I have a brain
Basketball is my favourite sport, I play it every day.

Jahanzaib Hussain (7)
The Godolphin Junior Academy, Slough

Magnificent Me

I like grumpy games
I like funky food
I like silly sleep
I love all of them.

I like fancy football
I like glory goals
I like legendary learning
I like scholarship schools
I love all of them.

Amna Saleem (10)
The Godolphin Junior Academy, Slough

This Is Me

I am cool as ice
I am cute as a bunny
I am fast as lightning
I am bright as the sun
I am brave as a lion
I am clear as a crystal ball
I am as smart as my mother.

Aadam Qazi (8)
The Godolphin Junior Academy, Slough

My Book On A Library Shelf

I love fantasy stories
And I also love to be on a stage
Full of rainbow lights
Once I had written a short story.
My daddy packed it like a real book
A fantasy princess in a wonderland
To Mrs Evans my teacher I went
To put my 'book' on the shelf
"No," said Mrs Evans
"Dear Janiel, don't worry, your book will get on a shelf someday."
She told me and I believe every word of it.

Janiel Ugbede (6)
The Rosary Catholic Primary School, Stroud

All About Me

If I told you all about me,
You can't explore with what you see,
So much to describe me or you,
Or anyone for that particular reason to,
Jet-black like gloves,
Not white like doves,
Dark brown skin,
Which could colour a pin,
Me, loving dinosaurs,
Which could be so much more.
Now I end the poem,
As I really want to say,
You were a great audience, okay.
This is me.

Sean C. Ike-Nwofor (9)
The Rosary Catholic Primary School, Stroud

I Am Glad To Be Me

If I didn't have CF I might be taller
My lungs would be stronger and my skin would not be salty
If I didn't have CF I wouldn't have so much medication to take,
I wouldn't have to go to the hospital all the time.
And I would have more time to play with my friends.
But CF is part of me, it makes me who I am.
I am glad to be me.

Mia Webb (7)
The Rosary Catholic Primary School, Stroud

While I Smile

My mum went to the shop while I smile at what she might buy
My dog jumped on a log while I laughed about it.
I saw a witch while I switched into a witch.
I said a rhyme while I played with slime.
I see a bee while I smile,
I went to school and I played with a ball while I laughed.
My dad has some wine and it was fine while I laughed.

Emma Neale (7)
The Rosary Catholic Primary School, Stroud

This Is Me

This is me
Free with my family
In the afternoon, after school, I change into my home clothes
Then I play and play and play until it's dinner time,
Before we read, we eat our tea.
When I go to bed I don't sleep well
So I wake up mostly late,
Others early
But I am free with my family.

Peniel Ugbede (7)
The Rosary Catholic Primary School, Stroud

Friend

K ind and happy
I nterested and impressive
N ice
D reamy

A nimal interested
N ice
D elicate

H appy
A mazing
P urple
P atient
Y ou.

Nadia Denis (7)
The Rosary Catholic Primary School, Stroud

Katy

K ind, thoughtful, loving
A lways ready for a cuddle
T rying new things, full of ideas
Y ou'll recognise me by my big smile, red hair, the smell of Mummy's washing.

Katy Watt (7)
The Rosary Catholic Primary School, Stroud

Abbie's Lovely Poem

A lways a good girl
B eing a good friend
B right colours make me happy
I 'm Mummy's sunny bunny
E veryone is nice to me.

Abbie Watt (5)
The Rosary Catholic Primary School, Stroud

The Hunter

A furry beast, stripes and spots on her thigh,
Surveys her kingdom from way up high.
Slim and athletic, a hunting machine,
She lurks in the shadows not to be seen.

Her attack's execution must be free of flaws,
She paws at the tree, sharpening her claws.
She switches her eyes from stealth mode to night,
Preparing her legs to pounce and take flight.

She crouches down low, ready for the kill,
She will execute it perfectly with hunter's skill.
Her prey violently shaking, it was too late
The predator had already sealed its fate.

With a twitch of the tail, and a mighty roar,
She topples her victim down to the floor.
Is this a tiger let loose in my house?
No, just my cat George and her vibrating mouse.

Elliott Carter (10)
Woodlands School, Great Warley

What Will I Be?

I'm asked one question you see,
Like when I'm older, what will I be?
They say, "How about working as a vet?
Studying hard, then rescuing pets."
But I could give them the wrong cure,
And there's no way to check for sure,
So I think I will pass on that one,
Although it could be very fun.
Some people say, "Why not a cook?
It can't be hard, it's all in a book.
There are so many things that you can take.
Some bread, some buns, a fairy cake."
But that's the thing I'll not enjoy
So I would be bad to employ.
Well, there's a teacher, builder, keeper of bees.
Are none of those a fit for me?
Is there nothing that I want to be,
A banker, a lawyer, an employee?
There is one job I would love to do,
A famous singer, yes it is true.
I'd sing all day, and sing all night,

Singing under dazzling light,
My fans would explode with roaring screams,
Finally, I have accomplished my lifelong dream.

Amelia Parker (10)
Woodlands School, Great Warley

Flower

I am like a flower,
My hair is like the petals gently rocking against the cool breeze,
My lips are as red as rose,
My cheeks are as pink as fresh summer flower blooming,
And my eyes are like bluebells.

I stand tall like the stem of a flower,
And my legs are as long as a tulip reaching for the sun,
In winter I am a Mahania and in spring I am a snowdrop,
I am a tulip in summer and a dahlia in autumn.

When I am sad I am a bluebell,
When I am happy I am a dahlia,
When I am droopy I am a snowdrop,
And when I am calm I am lavender.

Madeline Bolesworth (10)
Woodlands School, Great Warley

Swim Life

Hi, I am Thomas and I am a swimmer,
This is how I started off as a beginner,
I started at Hutton Manor School,
That is where I first set off in a pool.

Then to Killerwhales,
To Brentwood where I made many fails,
And after two years I was free,
I am now at Basildon club and they were quicker than me.

I was development two,
These people were my new crew,
I was sure of the ISA gold,
But my times weren't quick enough I was told.

Thomas William Ashby (10)
Woodlands School, Great Warley

This Is Me!

Sketching and drawing will never be boring
You won't hear me snoring
Sports is not my thing
But archery is my zing!

My cheeks are as red as a rose
And I have a very pink nose

I'm like a cute bunny that will fight
And never hesitate to bite
In the middle of the night
I feel a big fright
I go downstairs
To see if there are any scares.

Athena Bloom (10)
Woodlands School, Great Warley

My Favourite

She is the best of the best
A definite wonder
I am blessed
Usually wearing a bright pink jumper.

Hugging me day and night
She makes me very happy
She always makes everything just right,
She never gets snappy.

Now I wonder who she is
Oh bother;
She's not a he,
Because she's my mother.

Kieran Chantler (10)
Woodlands School, Great Warley

This Is Me: Football

F ootball is my thing
O liver is my name
O ranges are my favourite fruit
T ry very hard to be the best I can be
B ut my favourite thing is my family and friends
A lways a bit cheeky
L eft wing is my favourite position
L aughing, I always am.

Oliver Kerley (9)
Woodlands School, Great Warley

My Dog

My dog is Rocco,
He's only one,
Very crazy,
But lots of fun.

He runs around,
And barks a lot,
I give him treats,
But he'll never stop.

He's a funny cockapoo,
He will give you licks,
He'll run around the garden,
And then bring tiny sticks.

Bethany Conti (10)
Woodlands School, Great Warley

The Riddle

Chocolate melting in my mouth,
Gingerbread used to make a house,
Candy cane used to finish a house,
Jelly used for my blouse.

Passing by liquorice lagoon,
Looking at the gummy balloons,
I have no clue,
Now I'm in chocolate glue.

Joel Adegbite (11)
Woodlands School, Great Warley

YoungWriters®
Est. 1991

YOUNG WRITERS INFORMATION

We hope you have enjoyed reading this book – and that you will continue to in the coming years.

If you're the parent or family member of an enthusiastic poet or story writer, do visit our website **www.youngwriters.co.uk/subscribe** and sign up to receive news, competitions, writing challenges and tips, activities and much, much more! There's lots to keep budding writers motivated!

If you would like to order further copies of this book, or any of our other titles, then please give us a call or order via your online account.

Young Writers
Remus House
Coltsfoot Drive
Peterborough
PE2 9BF
(01733) 890066
info@youngwriters.co.uk

Join in the conversation!
Tips, news, giveaways and much more!

f YoungWritersUK **🐦** YoungWritersCW **📷** youngwriterscw